ISBN 978-0-364-55071-7
PIBN 11276062

1 MONTH OF
FREE
READING

at

www.ForgottenBooks.com

By purchasing this book you are eligible for one month membership to ForgottenBooks.com, giving you unlimited access to our entire collection of over 1,000,000 titles via our web site and mobile apps.

To claim your free month visit:

www.forgottenbooks.com/free1276062

English
Français
Deutsche
Italiano
Español
Português

www.forgottenbooks.com

Mythology Photography **Fiction**
Fishing Christianity **Art** Cooking
Essays Buddhism Freemasonry
Medicine **Biology** Music **Ancient
Egypt** Evolution Carpentry Physics
Dance Geology **Mathematics** Fitness
Shakespeare **Folklore** Yoga Marketing
Confidence Immortality Biographies
Poetry **Psychology** Witchcraft
Electronics Chemistry History **Law**
Accounting **Philosophy** Anthropology
Alchemy Drama Quantum Mechanics
Atheism Sexual Health **Ancient History**
Entrepreneurship Languages Sport
Paleontology Needlework Islam
Metaphysics Investment Archaeology
Parenting Statistics Criminology
Motivational

Historic, archived document

Do not assume content reflects current
scientific knowledge, policies, or practices.

H AND DEVELOPMENT

)ER COMPARED WITH CONIFERS

30-YEAR-OLD STANDS

BY CARL M. BERNTSEN

PACIFIC NORTHWEST
FOREST AND RANGE EXPERIMENT STATION
U.S. DEPT. OF AGRICULTURE · FOREST SERVICE

SUMMARY

Early interest in the management of red alder in the coastal forests of Oregon and Washington stimulated the start, in 1935, of a long-term stand-growth and development study. Two 1-acre plots and two half-acre plots were established on abandoned cleared land where 8- to 12-year-old stands of red alder and conifers were developing. The conifer component consisted of a mixture of Douglas-fir, Sitka spruce, and western hemlock. Selections and treatments brought about diversified composition of the experimental stands, as follows: (1) pure alder, unthinned, (2) mixed alder-conifer, unthinned, (3) pure alder, thinned from an alder-conifer stand at age 11 years, and (4) pure conifer, thinned from an alder-conifer stand at age 8.

Beginning in 1941, 5-year periodic measurements were made through the 1956 growing season to provide data for comparing growth between treatments and species. Major results were:

1. By age 29 years, the slow-starting pure conifer stand had about equalled the volume of the 32-year-old unthinned pure alder stand and had surpassed the yield of the thinned pure alder and unthinned alder-conifer stands.

2. Yield of the thinned pure alder stand at age 31 was about 13 percent less than that of the unthinned pure alder stand.

3. Yield of the unthinned alder-conifer stand at age 29 was the lowest of all experimental stands.

Results show that the conifer stand responded to release. In contrast, individual trees of the thinned pure alder stand showed negligible accelerated growth. This is interpreted to mean that the suppressed and perhaps intermediate trees in a pure, unthinned alder stand have only a minor effect on growth of the dominant and codominant trees. Lack of thinning in the alder-conifer stand, however, resulted in a prolonged struggle between species and a reduction in yield.

This publication is based on a thesis submitted to the School of Forestry, Oregon State College, in partial fulfillment of the requirements for the Master of Science degree. Work was done while the author was assigned to the Station's Corvallis Research Center, which is maintained in cooperation with the School of Forestry, Oregon State College.

Research Paper 38

GROWTH AND DEVELOPMENT OF RED ALDER

COMPARED WITH CONIFERS

IN 30-YEAR-OLD STANDS

by

Carl M. Berntsen

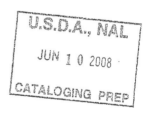

January 1961

PACIFIC NORTHWEST
FOREST AND RANGE EXPERIMENT STATION
R. W. Cowlin, Director   Portland, Oregon

FOREST SERVICE   U.S. DEPARTMENT OF AGRICULTURE

CONTENTS

INTRODUCTION

Red alder (Alnus rubra), although a widespread tree species in Pacific coast forests, has only in recent years attained commercial importance as a source of wood material for diversified products including furniture, paneling, and paper pulp. With the rapid increase in the harvest of red alder, both public agencies and private industry are making a real effort to develop at least tentative guidelines on how and where to grow red alder as a commercial timber crop.

Natural habitats of existing alder stands clearly illustrate conditions under which it grows and where it grows best, but knowledge is sketchy as to whether it is the best species for a particular site. To help provide basic growth data for red alder and associated species, experimental plots were established[1] during the period 1935-37 on the Cascade Head Experimental Forest, near the Oregon coast.

Treatments for this experiment were designed to illustrate potential growth of red alder as it occurs in pure stands, in mixture with conifers of the same age, and in stands thinned to pure alder at an early age. Growth of these alder stands was compared with growth of a stand thinned to pure conifer--Douglas-fir (Pseudotsuga menziesii), Sitka spruce (Picea sitchensis), and western hemlock (Tsuga heterophylla).

REVIEW OF LITERATURE

Some of the better known characteristics of red alder have been emphasized by other investigators. Johnson et al. (1926) stated: "Owing to its early maturity, the [conifer] species which are first suppressed by red alder later outstrip it." Haddock (1948-49) reported that dense 20- to 30-year-old stands have remarkably even crown canopies. Baker (1951) concluded that even-aged alder stands mature at 60 to 65 years of age. Another characteristic frequently discussed is the amelioration of site through the buildup of soil nitrogen and abundant leaf humus (Tarrant et al., 1951).[2]

---

[1] Persons instrumental in the planning and establishment of the study included Walter H. Meyer, Leo A. Isaac, Marion Nance, and Thornton T. Munger, all of the U.S. Forest Service.

[2] Also: Tarrant, Robert F. Stand development and soil fertility in a Douglas-fir—red alder plantation. 1960. (Manuscript accepted by Forest Sci. for publication.)

Not so universally understood is the development of red alder in mixed stands, nor the comparative production of red alder and conifers. The early theory that red alder provides a good nurse crop for other trees probably grew out of the use of other species of alder in Europe in planted stands of beech and oak (Haddock, 1948-49). This theory might hold true for a less competitive species of alder, or one out of its natural range, but there is little agreement among foresters that red alder serves as an effective nurse crop for conifers under natural development in Pacific coast forests. Instead, comments of the opposite opinion are more common. Aufderheide[3]/ stated: "Contrary to common belief, alder is not a good nurse crop for conifers. It is instead a rugged competitor." And Day (1957) remarked: "It seems to be quite certain that no species of conifer will become established where it /red alder/ occurs in really dense young thickets." Lloyd (1955), referring to productive capacity, estimated that Douglas-fir is about 38 percent more efficient as a wood producer than red alder on a similar site.

On the plus side, red alder has several features that readily adapt it to short-rotation management. Some of these are vigorous establishment on properly prepared sites (Haddock, 1948-49), rapid early growth (Johnson et al., 1926), and early maturity (Warrack, 1949). In short, it seems more logical to manage Pacific coast stands of red alder for production of wood than for its merits as a nurse crop or soil builder.

One of the biggest gaps in red alder information has been a lack of reliable methods for estimating yields. In part, this need has been recently met through the release of a new set of normal yield tables (Worthington et al., 1960), which apply to fully stocked stands of pure alder under natural development. Additional yield information is needed to help the forest manager decide not only which species to grow but also when to thin and harvest. This includes knowledge of the comparative yields of alder and conifer when grown on the same site and the development of yield information for mixed alder-conifer stands, for understocked stands, and eventually for managed stands.

---

[3]/ Aufderheide, Robert. Some notes on alder management. 1950. (Unpublished report on file at Pac. NW. Forest & Range Expt. Sta., U.S. Forest Serv., Portland, Oreg.)

DESCRIPTION OF STUDY AREA

At time of plot establishment, the study area, which covers a tract
pproximately 20 acres, was well stocked with red alder and conifer
roduction. The land had at one time been cleared for agriculture but
abandoned about 1925. Topography is relatively uniform, with moder-
slopes of about 15 percent and a generally southwesterly aspect. No
or water courses transect the study area, and the tract is site class III
Douglas-fir. Elevation is about 600 feet.

Soils in the vicinity are classified as Astoria silty clay loam, repre-
ative of the reddish-brown latosol suborder of the great soil groups.
depth ranges up to 6 feet and reaction is strongly acid, with a pH of
it 5.0. Because of the mild, wet climate, organic matter decomposes
dly. The forest floor is usually less than 2 inches thick, but the A_1
zon generally extends to 4 inches or more.

Climate is typical of the "fog belt"--a marine climate characterized
noderate temperatures, much cloudiness, frequent rains, and summer
Normal annual precipitation, almost all in the form of rain, is approx-
tely 90 inches. Mean summer and winter temperatures are about 68°
49° F., respectively. Days when the temperature is below freezing or
e 80° F. are infrequent (Ruth, 1954).

When the study plots were laid out, ground cover was fairly uniform,
western bracken (Pteridium aquilinum var. pubescens) the most com-
and rank species. Other conspicuous vegetation included rusty
ziesia (Menziesia ferruginea), salmonberry (Rubus spectabilis), St.
swort (Hypericum sp.), and fireweed (Epilobium angustifolium).
cken was especially dense in some areas, where it concealed conifer-
seedlings (fig. 1).

ire 1.--Ground cover conditions
hen the study was established in
35. Western bracken, partially
ertopped by red alder and a few
ouglas-firs, conceals almost
800 conifer seedlings per acre.

-3-

STAND TREATMENT AND PLOT ESTABLISHMENT

Altogether, four plots representing four stand conditions or treatments were established during the period 1935-37. These are:

1. Alder-conifer mixture, unthinned. -- This treatment is represented by a 1-acre plot established during June and July 1935. The stand--then 8 years old--contained almost 3,000 trees per acre, of which 60 percent were conifer and 40 percent alder (table 1). The plot was left unthinned as an example of natural development in a well-stocked stand of mixed alder and conifer.

2. Pure conifer, thinned. -- The 1/2-acre plot representing this treatment was established in March 1936. The original stand, also 8 years old, was similar in density

Table 1.--Number of trees per acre, by species, immediately following plot establishment and stand treatment

Stand treatment and minimum d.b.h. (inches)	Stand age	Trees per acre				
		Red alder	Douglas-fir	Sitka spruce	Western hemlock	Total
	Years	-----	-----	Number	-----	-----
Alder-conifer mixture (unthinned):						
0	8	1,208	362	1,292	133	2,995
1.5	do	239	2	0	0	241
Pure conifer (thinned):						
0	8	0	454	588	106	1,148
1.5	do	0	24	0	0	24
Pure alder (thinned):						
0	11	733	0	0	0	733
1.5	do	585	0	0	0	585
Pure alder (unthinned):[1]						
0	12	1,353	0	0	0	1,353
1.5	do	1,177	0	0	0	1,177

[1] Includes dominant, codominant, and intermediate red alders only; suppressed red alders and a few small conifers were not tallied.

and composition to the mixed alder-conifer stand of treatment 1 above. In this treatment, however, all alder trees were removed and the remaining conifers were thinned to a spacing of approximately 6 by 6 feet, leaving 1,148 trees per acre (table 1).

3. Pure alder, thinned. --This treatment is represented by a 1-acre plot established in April 1937. At that time the original stand was 11 years old and contained a mixture of alder and conifers much like the original stands of treatments 1 and 2 above. In this case, however, all conifers were removed and the remaining alders thinned to a spacing of about 8 by 8 feet, leaving 733 trees per acre (table 1).

4. Pure alder, unthinned. --A 1/2-acre plot established in April 1937 in a 12-year-old stand represents this treatment. Here the original stand was almost pure alder rather than an alder-conifer mixture as in treatments 1, 2, and 3. The stand was very well stocked and only red alders in the dominant, codominant, and intermediate crown classes were tallied. These totaled 1,353 per acre (table 1). The stand was left unthinned to represent the natural development of well-stocked red alder (fig. 2).

Figure 2. --The thinned (foreground) and the unthinned (right background) pure alder stands as they appeared after establishment in 1937.

DATA COLLECTION AND ANALYSIS

The first measurement after plot establishment was made in 1941, when the stands were 14 to 17 years old.[4] Thereafter, measurements were made every 5 years through 1956. Data recorded at each examination included tree diameters at breast height, mortality, and a representative sample of tree heights.

Although trees of all sizes were tallied at time of plot establishment, only those 1.5 inches d.b.h. and larger were measured at later dates or included in the analysis.

Trees were classified by 1-inch diameter classes, starting with the 2-inch class. In computing volume statistics, three distinct utilization standards were used, as follows:

1. Cubic volume of entire stem of all trees in the 2-inch diameter class or larger.

2. Cubic volume of all trees in the 6-inch diameter class or larger. Volume of top and stump excluded. This standard approximates commercial stand volumes under current utilization practices.

3. Board-foot volume (Scribner rule) of all trees in the 12-inch diameter class or larger.

The procedure outlined in "Standard Computations for Permanent Sample Plots" (Staebler, 1954) was used as a guide in preparing stand tables, height curves, and local volume tables. For the most part, published volume tables (U.S. Forest Service, 1953) were used in preparing local tables, but some adjustments were necessary. Cubic volumes of the red alder table had to be extended downward to include diameters of 2 inches and heights of 20 feet. In addition, volumes for the stump and top had to be added in computing total tree volume for trees in the 2-inch diameter class or larger. The lower diameter classes of the cubic-foot Sitka spruce table were also adjusted to appear more reasonable when curved. All these adjustments have been incorporated in revised volume tables, published in 1959 (Skinner).

---

[4] Stand ages vary slightly from calendar dating to conform to number of growing seasons. For example, the pure conifer stand was estimated to be 8 years old when established in March 1936. Five years later, in September 1941, age of this stand was recorded as 14 years because six growing seasons had elapsed. Ages of the two pure alder stands were likewise adjusted to a growing-season base.

RESULTS AND DISCUSSION

Number of Trees

Initial stand treatments created a wide variation in composition and number of trees (table 1). During the course of stand development, however, principal interest has gradually changed from total number to number of trees in the larger diameter classes (fig. 3).

Total number of trees culminated at about age 16 in the pure alder stands compared with age 19 in the alder-conifer mixture and age 24 in the pure conifer stand.

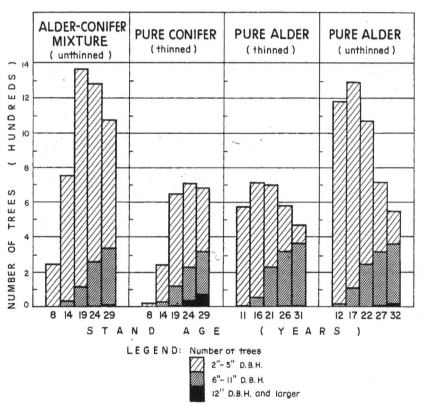

Figure 3. --During the study, the total number of trees per acre (entire bar) has varied considerably among stand treatments. In contrast, number of trees in the 6-inch d.b.h. class and larger has been fairly uniform among treatments.

At the last examination, number of trees in the 6-inch class and larger varied only from 320 per acre in the pure conifer stand to 362 in the unthinned pure alder stand.

Tree Heights

Average tree heights have varied considerably with stand composition (fig. 4). At a common stand age of 29 years, average heights were 57 and 49 feet for alder and conifers, respectively, in the alder-conifer mixture; 59 feet in the pure conifer; 63 feet in the thinned pure alder; and 70 feet in the unthinned pure alder. The removal of some of the taller trees and perhaps several of the potentially faster growing seedlings in the original thinning of the pure alder may account for the greater average tree heights in the unthinned pure alder stand.

Although thinned and unthinned pure alder maintained their initial height advantage over the pure conifer (due to earlier seedling establishment and rapid juvenile height growth of alder), rate of height growth among the three stand treatments was about equal throughout the entire period of study.

Cubic Volume

At the time of the last examination, cubic-foot volume for both the 2- and 6-inch utilization standards was greatest in the unthinned pure alder stand and second greatest in the pure conifer stand (table 2). The 1956 volume of the pure conifer stand for trees in the 2-inch diameter class and larger is impressive considering that it contained 2,400 cubic feet less than the unthinned pure alder at the time of the 1946 measurement. The conifer stand has gained volume very rapidly in the last 10 years. For the 6-inch standard, the difference between the two stands at the time of the last examination was only 248 cubic feet.

When volumes shown in table 2 were curved to make comparisons on an equal-age basis, differences between alder plots were reduced and the favorable position of the pure conifer stand was strengthened. At a common age of 29 years, volume (2-inch d.b.h. class and larger) of the pure conifer stand matched the 4,600 cubic feet of the unthinned pure alder (fig. 5a). For trees in the 6-inch d.b.h. class and larger (fig. 5b), cubic-foot volumes in the pure conifer overtook the unthinned pure alder at age 27 and built up a 500-cubic-foot margin by age 29. This difference was slightly greater than the margin at age 29 of the unthinned pure alder over the thinned pure alder and the thinned pure alder over the alder-conifer mixture. Release of alder by removing the conifers apparently minimized the competitive struggle between species that occurred in the unthinned alder-conifer mixture. A comparison of the thinned and unthinned alder stands indicates, however, that more growing stock than necessary was removed in the thinned stand.

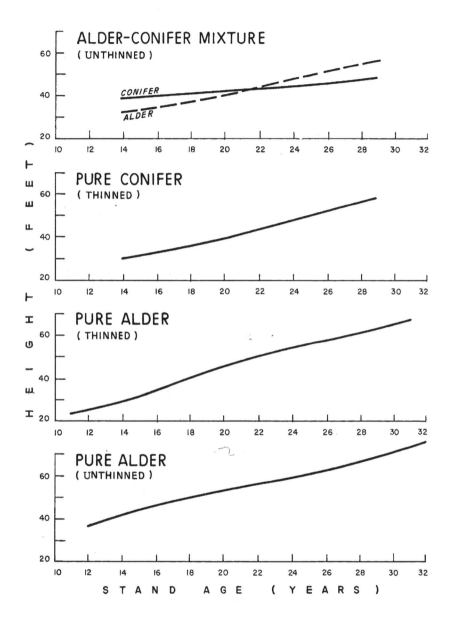

Figure 4. --Average heights of all trees in the 6-inch d.b.h. class and larger.

Table 2.--Cubic-foot volume per acre by stand treatment

and year of measurement

Stand treatment and minimum diameter class (inches)[1]	Range in stand age during study	Year of measurement					
		1935	1937	1941	1946	1951	1956
	Years	---------------- Cubic feet ----------------					
Alder-conifer mixture (unthinned):							
2	8-29	164	--	679	1,732	2,943	3,970
6	do	0	--	100	452	1,490	2,705
Pure conifer (thinned):							
2	8-29	3	--	208	1,018	2,641	4,736
6	do	0	--	81	584	1,877	3,880
Pure alder (thinned):							
2	11-31	--	455	1,219	2,427	3,340	4,335
6	do	--	8	176	1,263	2,319	3,539
Pure alder (unthinned):							
2	12-32	--	1,165	2,486	3,424	4,196	5,155
6	do	--	67	539	1,626	2,796	4,128

[1] The 2-inch diameter class and larger includes volume of tip above 4 inches d.i.b. and stump. The 6-inch class and larger does not include stump and tip volume.

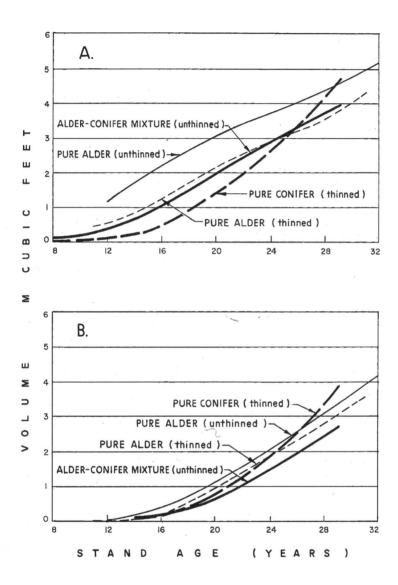

Figure 5.--Cubic-foot volume per acre: A, 2-inch d.b.h. class and larger; B, 6-inch d.b.h. class and larger. Curves were made by smoothing lines between points of periodic volume estimates (table 2).

Board-Foot Volume

At the time of the most recent measurement (1956), board-foot volumes per acre (Scribner rule), including only those trees in the 12-inch d.b.h. class or larger, were:

Stand treatment:	Stand age (Years)	Trees (Number)	Volume (Bd. ft.)
Alder-conifer mixture (unthinned)	29	13	1, 295
Pure conifer (thinned)	29	74	6, 714
Pure alder (thinned)	31	6	648
Pure alder (unthinned)	32	20	2, 538

The good response of the conifer stand to release thinning at age 8 years is clearly expressed in the large number of trees in the 12-inch d.b.h. class and larger, as well as in its unmatched board-foot volume. Although the other stand treatments may improve their board-foot production during the next measurement period through ingrowth, the board-foot production of the pure conifer stand will probably never be equalled because of its 1956 superiority in average diameter, shown by d.b.h. class (inches) in the following tabulation:

Stand treatment:	Stand age (Years)	D.b.h. class 6 to 11 (Inches)	12+ (Inches)
Alder-conifer mixture (unthinned)	29	7.8	12.7
Pure conifer (thinned)	29	8.5	13.8
Pure alder (thinned)	31	7.9	12.5
Pure alder (unthinned)	32	8.0	12.8

Growth

The growth terms used in this report are compatible with terms listed in Forestry Terminology (Society of American Foresters, 1958) and are defined as follows:

> Ingrowth. Volume at end of measurement period of trees that grew into the minimum-diameter class during the period.

> Net increment. Volume of live trees at end of measurement period (including ingrowth)

minus volume of live trees at start of meas‑
urement period.

Mortality. Volume at beginning of measurement
period of trees that died during the measure‑
ment period.

Gross increment. Net increment plus mortality.

Net increment is expressed in terms of both periodic annual incre‑
ment and mean annual increment--total growth divided by total age. All
four growth elements are expressed in terms of periodic annual increment--
growth for any specified period divided by number of years in the period.

Mean annual net increment. --Mean annual net increment in cubic
feet per acre increased throughout the measurement period for all stand
treatments, as shown in the following tabulation:

		Mean annual net increment	
	Stand age	2 inches + d.b.h.	6 inches + d.b.h.
	(Years)	(Cu. ft.)	(Cu. ft.)
Stand treatment:			
Alder-conifer mixture (unthinned)	8	20	0
	14	48	7
	19	91	24
	24	122	62
	29	137	93
Pure conifer (thinned)	8	0	0
	14	15	6
	19	54	31
	24	110	78
	29	163	134
Pure alder (thinned)	11	41	1
	16	76	11
	21	116	60
	26	128	89
	31	140	114
Pure alder (unthinned)	12	97	6
	17	146	32
	22	156	74
	27	155	104
	32	161	129

The pure conifer stand, though starting slowly, grew rapidly after age 14 years, and by age 29 had surpassed all other treatments. Mean annual increment of the pure conifer stand has, moreover, continued to increase at a steady rate in contrast to the slackening pace of the pure alder stands.

Periodic annual net increment. --Periodic annual net increment in the 2-inch d.b.h. class and larger culminated before the age of 25 years for all stands except the pure conifer, which continued to increase through age 29 (table 3, fig. 6a). Culmination in the 6-inch d.b.h. class and larger, however, had not occurred in any of the four stand conditions at

Table 3.--Periodic annual increment and mortality per acre,

by stand treatment and stand age period

Stand treatment and age period (years)	2-inch d.b.h. class and larger[1]				6-inch d.b.h. class and larger[2]			
	In-growth	Net increment	Mor-tality	Gross increment	In-growth	Net increment	Mor-tality	Gross increment
	--- Cubic feet ---							
Alder-conifer mixture (unthinned):								
8-14	44	86	0	86	17	17	0	17
14-19	38	210	0	210	56	70	0	70
19-24	2	242	22	264	128	208	0	208
24-29	2	206	56	262	68	243	1	244
Pure conifer (thinned):								
8-14	19	34	0	34	13	13	0	13
14-19	30	162	0	162	65	101	0	101
19-24	7	325	14	339	86	259	13	272
24-29	3	419	3	422	81	401	0	401
Pure alder (thinned):								
11-16	19	153	0	153	30	34	0	34
16-21	1	241	3	244	172	217	0	217
21-26	0	183	34	217	131	211	0	211
26-31	2	198	52	250	61	244	5	249
Pure alder (unthinned):								
12-17	18	264	2	266	82	94	0	94
17-22	6	188	38	226	135	237	0	237
22-27	0	154	79	233	77	234	3	237
27-32	12	192	86	278	50	266	0	266

[1]Total tree volume, including tip above 4 inches d.i.b. and stump.

[2]Excludes tip above 4 inches d.i.b. and stump.

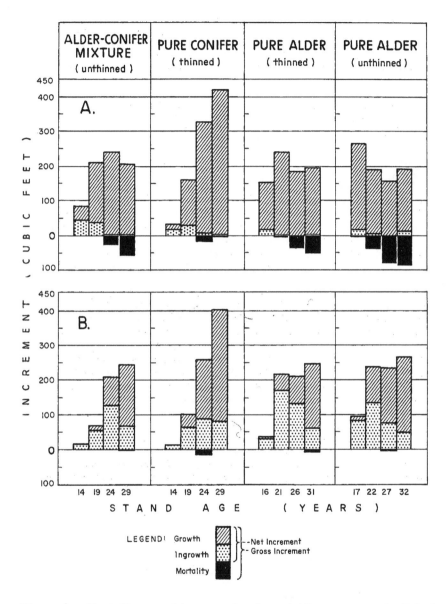

Figure 6.--Periodic annual increment and mortality per acre: A, 2-inch
d.b.h. class and larger; B, 6-inch d.b.h. class and larger. Most mortality occurred in the 2- to 6-inch d.b.h. classes.

the time of last examination. But here, too, the pure conifer stand has greatly outproduced all other treatments since age 19 (table 3, fig. 6b). At time of last examination, periodic annual net increment for the pure conifer was 401 cubic feet per acre, compared to a range of only 243 to 266 for the other stand treatments. The unthinned pure alder stand ranked second.

For all stand treatments, ingrowth into the 6-inch d.b.h. class has accounted for a substantial part of the periodic annual net increment during all measurement periods (fig. 6b).

Composition

Trends in species composition varied markedly among stand treatments (table 4). The pure alder stands remained practically pure alder, and the pure conifer stand contained only 5 percent red alder at age 29 (fig. 7). The pure conifer stand, however, gradually changed from pure Douglas-fir to a mixed stand with increasing amounts of Sitka spruce and western hemlock. The stand will probably remain predominantly Douglas-fir, but the proportion of spruce and hemlock is likely to increase.

The most pronounced change in composition took place in the alder-conifer mixture. Here, the presence of a large number of coniferous seedlings was not reflected in the initial volume estimate at age 8 because the conifers were too small to be inventoried. Although initial development of the conifers was slow, by age 29 they made up about one-quarter of the stand volume. Much of the conifer volume consists of small trees that persisted under the alder canopy. The conifers will doubtless form a much more prominent component of the stand after the alder overstory opens up.

APPLICATION

Results of this study may have regionwide application but should be used with discretion because of the case-history nature of the data. Some relationships, however, appear clear cut and may suggest use in common practice.

For example, the yield of a 30-year-old conifer stand will probably equal or exceed that of a 30-year-old alder stand on the same site and thereafter greatly outproduce it. A logical silvicultural treatment in a young stand of mixed alder-conifer, therefore, would be to convert to a higher producing conifer stand by removing the alders. Since the conifers respond better to precommercial thinning than the alder, this practice would also facilitate a later program of commercial thinning.

In contrast, if a young, fully stocked alder stand contains little or no conifers in mixture, it would seem more prudent to delay conversion to a conifer stand until the alder can be harvested in a clear-cutting operation. Since little or no release occurs in alder stands from removal of the lower crown class trees, thinning would be used primarily to salvage dead and dying trees of commercial size.

Table 4.--Stand composition in percentage of cubic-foot volume,

by stand treatment and stand age

Stand treatment and stand age (years)	Red alder		Douglas-fir		Sitka spruce		Western hemlock	
	2 in.+	6 in.+	2 in.+	6 in.+	2 in.+	6 in.+	2 in.+	6 in.+
	------------------------- Percent -----------------------							
Alder-conifer mixture (unthinned):								
8	100	0	(1/)	0	0	0	0	0
14	93	87	6	13	1	0	(1/)	0
19	81	79	10	21	8	0	1	0
24	75	78	11	17	12	3	2	2
29	73	78	12	15	13	5	2	2
Pure conifer (thinned):								
8	0	0	100	0	0	0	0	0
14	0	0	97	100	2	0	1	0
19	2	0	80	97	15	2	3	1
24	4	2	71	83	21	11	4	4
29	5	5	68	73	22	17	5	5
Pure alder (thinned):								
11	100	100	0	0	0	0	0	0
16	100	100	0	0	0	0	0	0
21	100	100	0	0	0	0	0	0
26	100	100	0	0	0	0	0	0
31	100	100	0	0	(1/)	0	0	0
Pure alder (unthinned):								
12	100	100	0	0	0	0	0	0
17	100	100	0	0	0	0	0	0
22	100	100	0	0	0	0	0	0
27	100	100	0	0	0	0	0	0
32	99	100	0	0	1	(1/)	0	0

1/Less than 0.5 percent.

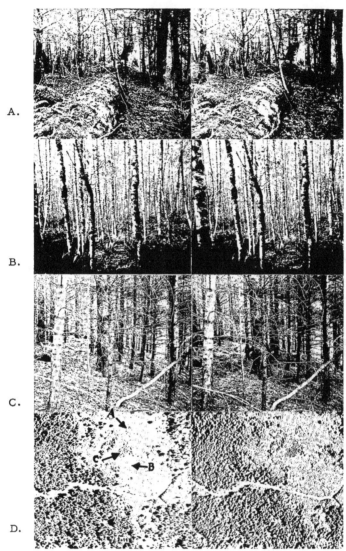

Figure 7.--Stereogram of study area and stand treatments about 20 years
after treatment: A, Unthinned alder-conifer mixture at age 29 years;
B, ·thinned pure alder at age 31; C, thinned pure conifer at age 29;
D, aerial view of study tract and surrounding 100-year-old stand of
Sitka spruce, western hemlock, and Douglas-fir, showing location of
stand treatments.

LITERATURE CITED

Baker, William J.
    1951. Some factors involved in the promotion of alder-using indus-
        tries in Tillamook, Oregon. Oreg. Forest Prod. Lab.
        Spec. Rpt. 1, 35 pp.

Day, W. R.
    1957. Sitka spruce in British Columbia. Forestry Comm. Bul. 28,
        110 pp., illus. London.

Haddock, Philip G.
    1948-49. A problem child reforms; new perspectives in the manage-
        ment of red alder. Univ. Wash. Forest Club Quart. 22(2):
        9-15.

Johnson, Herman M., Hanzlik, Edward J., and Gibbons, William H.
    1926. Red alder of the Pacific Northwest: its utilization, with notes
        on growth and management. U. S. Dept. Agr. Bul. 1437,
        46 pp., illus.

Lloyd, William J.
    1955. Alder thinning--progress report. U. S. Soil Conserv. Serv.
        Woodland Conserv. Tech. Notes 3, 6 pp. (Processed.)

Ruth, Robert H.
    1954. Cascade Head climatological data 1936-1952. U. S. Forest
        Serv. Pac. NW. Forest and Range Expt. Sta., 29 pp.
        (Processed.)

Skinner, Edgel C.
    1959. Cubic volume tables for red alder and Sitka spruce. U. S.
        Forest Serv. Pac. NW. Forest and Range Expt. Sta. Res.
        Note 170, 4 pp. (Processed.)

Society of American Foresters.
    1958. Forestry terminology. 97 pp. Washington, D. C.

Staebler, George R.
    1954. Standard computations for permanent sample plots. U. S.
        Forest Serv. Pac. NW. Forest and Range Expt. Sta.,
        15 pp. (Processed.)

Tarrant, Robert F., Isaac, Leo A., and Chandler, Robert F., Jr.
    1951. Observations on litter fall and foliage nutrient content of some
        Pacific Northwest tree species. Jour. Forestry 49: 914-915.

U.S. Forest Service.
    1953. Volume tables for permanent sample plots. U.S. Forest
        Serv. Pac. NW. Forest and Range Expt. Sta., 28 tables.
        (Processed.)

Warrack, George.
    1949. Treatment of red alder in the coastal region of British
        Columbia. Brit. Columbia Forest Serv. Res. Notes 14,
        7 pp. (Processed.)

Worthington, Norman P., Johnson, Floyd A., Staebler, George R., and
    Lloyd, William J.
    1960. Normal yield tables for red alder. U.S. Forest Serv. Pac.
        NW. Forest and Range Expt. Sta. Res. Paper 36, 3 pp.,
        13 tables.